This simple, colourful book introduces young children to the concept of **opposites**.

Illustrated in a lively, humorous style, **big and little** *deals with the words which describe relative sizes and positions, all shown through objects and scenes which will be familiar to young children.*

With very young children, we recommend that books are used with adult supervision.

British Library Cataloguing in Publication Data

Murdock, Hy
    Big and little. — Rev.
    1. Sizes
    I. Title   II. Wells, Tony   III. Series
    516
    ISBN 0-7214-1189-4

First edition

Published by Ladybird Books Ltd Loughborough Leicestershire UK
Ladybird Books Inc Auburn Maine 04210 USA

Printed in England

big and little

by HY MURDOCK
illustrated by TONY WELLS

Ladybird Books

Things have different shapes and sizes.

Some animals are **big**,
some animals are **little**.

Some people are **big**,
some are **middle-sized**
and some are **little**.

All around us we see **large** things and **small** things.

Here are some more
shapes and sizes.

A **thin**
clown

A **fat** clown

A **tall** king

A **short** king

A **long** dragon

A **short** dragon

We find things in lots
of different positions.

The see-saw
goes **up**
and **down**.

The boy rides
his bicycle
down the hill.

The man
pushes his bicycle
up the hill.

Incy Wincy spider,
climbing **up** the
spout.
Down came the rain
and washed the
spider out.
Out came the sun,
dried up all the rain.
Incy Wincy spider,
climbing **up** again.

We put our clothes **on** in the morning.

We take them **off** at bedtime.

The boy paints **high** up.

The girl paints **low** down.

A **high** shelf

A **low** shelf

The children play **indoors**...

and **outdoors**.

Jack is **in** the box.

Jack is **out** of the box.